Deconstructing My Fairy Tale

A Memoir

Grace Carrington

Edited by
Driadonna Roland

Deconstructing My Fairy Tale
A Memoir

iUniverse books may be ordered through booksellers or by contacting:

iUniverse
1663 Liberty Drive
Bloomington, IN 47403
www.iuniverse.com
1-800-Authors (1-800-288-4677)

Because of the dynamic nature of the Internet, any web addresses or
links contained in this book may have changed since publication and
may no longer be valid. The views expressed in this work are solely those
of the author and do not necessarily reflect the views of the publisher,
and the publisher hereby disclaims any responsibility for them.

Any people depicted in stock imagery provided by Thinkstock are
models, and such images are being used for illustrative purposes only.
Certain stock imagery © Thinkstock.

ISBN: 978-1-4917-5553-2 (sc)
ISBN: 978-1-4917-5554-9 (e)

Library of Congress Control Number: 2014922191

Printed in the United States of America.

iUniverse rev. date: 01/05/2015

Dedication

I dedicate this book to my daughters.
You are my pride and joy.
I love you bigger bigger!

Introduction

This book is a memoir of over a decade of my life. It begins with a fairy tale illusion conceived in my mind and perhaps my heart at the time. It ends with my reality and restoration. It begins with a young, emotionally out of control girl and ends with a mature mother of two.

I believe we create storylines and characters in our hearts and minds. We find comfort playing out our parts and assigning the blame to our villains. We set the stage for our heroes to save us. We spend days, nights, months, and even years making it all look good on the outside. While we are so busy telling ourselves that the fairy tale is real, we cannot fathom or understand when it all comes crashing down.

Perhaps it's because we have ignored all the red flags — or in my case the burning bushes. We have rationalized and intellectualized our bullshit, to the point where we believe it all. We believe that the story will end happily ever after despite the drama. More sadly, we believe we have control over how it ends.

No matter who we are or what we are, we all want love and to be loved. We hear the fairy tale stories as little girls and then watch the romantic comedies as young adults and even grown women. We desire for the storyline to be our real life. We want to believe magically that *Love Actually* will happen to us. So we as women, through no fault of our own, go to great lengths to make love happen. We are quicker to compromise and/or sacrifice our selves, careers, and lives for that love. So we pursue our love stories. I have learned there are many different variations of the fairy tale. Ultimately, we all want the happily ever after.

When our fairy tale ends, we are distraught not because the fairy tale has ended, but because we are embarrassed, ashamed, hurt, and confused. Confused because we have told ourselves the fairy tale is real and true over and over again. The mind is perplexed when it then has to operate from a basis of truth.

I will share with you my personal journey, from my fairy tale illusion to my authentic restoration. Told like a true Greek tragedy — as I know it, lived it, and believed it to be true.

There are many reasons I have chosen to write this book. The number one reason is to spare anyone from all the pain, heartache, and misery that I endured over the years of living in my fairy tale life. I tell this story for all young women so that they may live their life in truth, especially my daughters. I promise you that when you are done with this book, you will have a very clear understanding of the importance of being true to who you are. More important, you will learn that you must first be healthy and whole before you can truly love anyone.

Table of Contents

CHAPTER 1

"What's the matter with you; your fingers broken?"

It all started in my hometown of Newark, New Jersey circa 1999. I had just graduated from college with a bachelor's degree in management science. I was a young, single, independent girl doing my thing. I was working full time, making good money for my first job out of college — with benefits. A random encounter with a charming and handsome man led me to take a risk, leave my secure job, and go manage a café. This man was one of the owners. He persuaded me that managing the café would be an opportunity to connect with key players in the city of Newark. My focus would be management; implementing and overseeing live entertainment for the café. I had always wanted to open a restaurant. I figured I would get the experience using someone else's capital.

One day walking down the street to the café, I bumped into "Mr. LC," a friend of my uncle's. I smiled and said, "Hi, its Gracie — Kendall's niece." He looked back at me confused, and then said, "Oh… Gracie." We exchanged polite small talk and I told him I was managing this café and that he should stop in some time. We said goodbye and I thought to myself, "*I probably won't see him again, unless he's with my uncle.*"

Well to my surprise, about a week or so later he stopped in and bought an oatmeal cookie. Again, we exchanged greetings, and he kept it moving. This went on for several weeks. Finally at one of the spoken word poetry events, he asked for my telephone number. I said to myself, "*Oh why not? He's harmless.*" He was nothing like the men that I was accustomed to dating. So we exchanged numbers.

About two weeks went by and he still had not called. At that point, I was just annoyed at the fact that he hadn't called. I thought, "*Who the hell does he think he is to ask for my number and not call me?*" So I called him. This darling, is where the fairy tale begins. He picked up and I said, "What's the matter with you; your fingers broken?" He replied, "Oh no I'm sick, I've been sick." Then I replied, "Well maybe one day when you get better, we'll go out?" Well as you can imagine he got better. We scheduled and went on our first date.

God, those were the days! My entourage and I would always double-book ourselves for the night; usually dinner with some "nice guy" and polite conversation. After dinner, we gave the classic line, "I had an amazing time, but I'm gonna call it a night," which translated to, "*You were not the main event of the evening, you were at best the appetizer.*" Then, us girls would meet up and head into "the city" (Manhattan), always with the same agenda to drink and party with the rock stars and bad boys.

We never went to a club before midnight. We were always on the VIP guest list, having bottle service with the "ballers and shot callers." After the club, it was breakfast at the diner to recap the highlights of the night and our shenanigans. We advised each other on which one of the guys we should actually talk to when they called us. Back then they all called, so we always had options. Then we would head home, pass out, wake up, and do it all over again the next night. That was my life: young, sexy, single, and carefree. Our motto was work hard, play harder. I loved and enjoyed every minute of that lifestyle — it was intoxicating and addictive. Our social calendars were filled with rooftop parties and art gallery openings in SoHo. We were regulars at Tribeca Grill and had seats opening night at most of the Broadway plays. It was the quintessential life of a Manhattanite.

However, date night with Mr. LC went a little differently. At dinner, I asked, "So what's wrong with you, why are you still single?" Although I don't remember his response verbatim, I do know it was just the beginning of a decade of lies.

He charmed me so much that I canceled on my girl TJ. After dinner we went for drinks, which was a big no-no, unless it was with the main guy. Now don't get me wrong; I was always a juggler. I firmly believed in keeping your options open. Trust and believe I was still smitten with the slick-talking attorney who persuaded me to manage the café. We were dating at the time. Not to mention my ex-boyfriend, Mr. Rico. We dated off and on for five years. Mr. Rico was an engineer and super sexy. He was fun loving and we had lots of fun together — some nights too much fun. He was very good to me, especially during my college years. I thought we would eventually get married.

I wasn't completely sold on Mr. LC. I kept thinking, *He seems like such a "nice guy."* But I decided to keep him in the mix. However, it would be tricky. Mr. LC was one of my uncle's closest friends, and 10 years my senior.

Although I didn't know all the clinical terms, I knew I had always struggled with different emotions and feelings back then. I will never forget the night Mr. LC and I went to see *Girl, Interrupted*. I remember crying on our way back to my mother's house. There was a part of me that could relate to and identify with the characters' dysfunction, largely due to my childhood. I kept thinking, "*Wow, he is such a normal guy. I'm just as crazy as one of those characters in the movie.*"

I told him I needed to take my time with him and that I wasn't ready for anything serious. I was still trying to get over Mr. Rico. Mr. LC said all the right things and I believed every last word. I remember thinking, "*I'd be an idiot to pass up on this great guy!*"

You know, the kind of guy who wants to be with you on both the good and bad days. One time while we were dating, I got sick with a head cold. I canceled our plans to see each other that night. Shortly after we hung up the phone, my doorbell rang. It was Mr. LC with orange juice, soup, and cough drops. That small act blew me away. I had always dated the "Mr. Bigs." Those are the powerhouse businessmen, lawyers, engineers, etc. Although dating those guys had its advantages, it was always on their terms. After all, you were just another beautiful possession, like their penthouse apartment, sports car, and designer watches. The reality is even pretty faces with brains are always replaceable to the Mr. Bigs of the world.

As Mr. LC and I continued to date, I decided to put him in the number one slot. The reality is we women love a project. My friends and I referred to it as a "Bennifer" (Jennifer Lopez + Ben Affleck). You know how it goes: We meet a guy, probably average. Over time, we change his style of clothes, his social circle, and his overall lifestyle. After J.Lo was done with Ben Affleck he was almost unrecognizable. He had gone from wearing T-shirts and baseball caps to custom-made designer suits. So sexy! That's exactly what I did for Mr. LC.

It wasn't long after that Mr. LC told me he didn't want to just date me, he wanted to marry me. To test how serious he was, I wanted him to take us on vacation. I wanted to see if he could fit in with my lifestyle. I lived in France during college and traveled frequently with family and friends. So we took a couple of trips, South Beach and Cozumel, to be exact. It was during our vacation in South Beach that he officially asked me to marry him. No ring, just some poem he wrote that went something like this:

"I love you, I love you, I love you. I don't want to bore you with it." I said yes. In February 2000, on a hot South Beach Miami night, I was engaged to Mr. LC. At the time, he was my Prince Charming. He said all the things that Mr. Rico never said, and probably never felt.

I later found out that the words from the poem were from a Stevie Wonder song.

Chapter 2

The original platinum wedding

Mothers always know. My mother tried to warn me. In hindsight, save me! She said, "What is the rush, are you pregnant?" I said no. She said, "He's not like you, he doesn't like the things you like; you like the city, and going out. Plus he has a son. I never wanted you to marry someone with baby momma drama." I had never even dated anyone with a kid. I felt that he would be a suitable mate. After all, I had completed my project. He was now dressing the way I wanted —button-down shirts — we were going to comedy shows and plays, etc. I had fully acclimated Mr. LC into my world. Really, I was obsessed with having a spectacular wedding.

Well this was the year 2000, and it was all about the bling bling, baby! I had picked out this beautiful engagement ring. It was very expensive. I specifically told Mr. LC, "If you can't afford the ring, it's OK. I will pick out a smaller diamond." He replied, "No, I can handle it." Of course, being the total control freak I was I had instructions regarding the proposal. First, I told him that he would have to officially get on his knee and ask for my hand in marriage. Secondly he had to get my parents' blessing. I also told Mr. LC I didn't want some crazy romantic proposal. I was too cool for that corny stuff. I wanted something really laidback and intimate. He proposed on the night of my cousin's senior prom. I was at home rushing to get dressed to go to my cousin's house. I turned around, and there he was, on one knee. It was the prettiest diamond ring I had ever seen: a two-carat round VVSI diamond in a one-carat platinum setting. I remember thinking, *"Well it took you long enough to get my ring."* I was planning a wedding and didn't even have a ring on my finger.

Well, I later found out he borrowed money from his brother to help buy my ring. His family informed me that Mr. LC borrowed $7,000 from his brother; never paid him back. To his credit he did everything for his family, but you don't borrow $7,000 and never pay it back. That's just wrong. Honestly, I would have never taken the ring had I known he had to borrow from family.

Surely, you are thinking, *Well why did you pick out such an expensive engagement ring?* The answer is very simple: I knew my worth and I was accustomed to a certain lifestyle. After all, isn't that how a man shows his love for his future wife?

I will be the first to admit I was bridezilla from day one. It's funny because I was never that little girl who dreamed of her wedding day. Never did I sit and daydream of ideas about what that day would look like. Secretly, I questioned if I would ever get married, largely because of my childhood baggage. However, planning a wedding is like getting sucked into this narcissistic whirlwind tornado. I just started kicking ass and taking names. Anyone who didn't kiss my ass was on my list. Oh wait — that was just my personality back then. Sad but true, because I was not spiritually grounded. I had tantrum after tantrum, sprinkled with several emotional meltdowns during the wedding planning process, which included crying hysterically when the bridesmaid shoes were accidently dyed peach and my color was champagne. I called all the bridesmaids and demanded that they listen to my crying. I even threatened to call the Better Business Bureau on the shoe store. I was a piece of work! It got so out of control; I kicked one bridesmaid out of the wedding because she was late for a dress fitting. I have no idea exactly how many tantrums and meltdowns occurred during the year and a half of the planning stage. Let's just say there were so many that I earned a new nickname, "Gigi," aka Gully Girl. As I got older I realized many of those meltdowns were due to my inability to regulate my own emotions and had very little to do with being a bridezilla.

The date was set and plans were underway. Sounds good, right? Wrong! There were major red flags, which happened between the proposal and the wedding date of June 23, 2001. This was the cycle: I always called Mr. LC on his bullshit, he apologized, and I chose to rationalize and justify his "little white lies." After all, what's more important: having a platinum wedding or paying attention to the red flags of the person you are planning to spend the rest of your life with? Had I paid full attention to the issues and concerns, I wouldn't have been able to write this book. Actually, I take that back. I probably would have, just with a different name of the evil villain. I have acknowledged it was my choice to pursue the fairy tale and not the reality of the red flags.

So you are probably wondering what some of the red flags were. Well here are just a few, to give you the idea of how bright they were. First red flag was that Mr. LC's car windows were repeatedly busted out. Although Mr. LC lived in Newark, New Jersey, which was car theft capital of the country back in the '90s, people just do not have their windows busted over and over again. Well this happened three times, to be exact. I kept asking him, "Why does this keep happening to your car?" He said, "I don't know why." His mother eventually told me that it was his baby momma who was busting his car windows.

Second red flag was when Mr. LC said he wanted to "be the provider" and pay my bills. After the first month of him paying my bills I received all my statements with late charges. Now, I had excellent credit and always paid my bills on time. When I asked him, "Did you mail these on time?" I saw the face I would see a hundred times over the next ten years. With that pitiful lying face, he said, "Yes." Needless to say, from that point on I just got the money from him and mailed my own bills.

While Mr. LC was courting me, we had many conversations about what we wanted out of life, our likes, dislikes, how we wanted to raise our children, and so on. One of our chats regarded my appreciation of wine. He said he loved wine. Well one of the biggest reasons the marriage failed was because Mr. LC grossly misrepresented himself. So red flag number 15 was the fact that we were not even married and he had stopped drinking wine completely. All that so-called "talking" was in vain. It was nothing more than just him yessing me to death and saying what he knew I wanted to hear.

Lastly, my favorite red flag was when Mr. LC pretended he bought my first Mercedes Benz. My Honda Accord had gotten stolen from in front of his house. Of course, I'm sure you're not surprised. I wanted a car that could not be stolen, so I decided to buy my first Mercedes. Now it was my FICO score, my down payment that bought that car. (Just ask Ray Catena Financial Department.) However, Mr. LC took credit on several different occasions for being the one who purchased my car. It was my alleged engagement present. At the time, I did not have the heart to confront him and say that it bothered me. I loved him, but it never sat well with me that he felt the need to lie to make himself look good. I had no idea that would be my life over the next ten years: his lies.

Now, to be completely fair to myself, I had serious concerns regarding those red flags and the long-term ramifications. Shortly before the wedding, I met my good friend Ella at Dunkin' Donuts on Broad Street in Newark. I cried to her, saying, "I do not want to marry him." She was extremely supportive. I valued her insight and knew that her words were coming from a place of love and maturity. Together we tried to decipher whether it was typical last-minute jitters or whether I should listen to the pit in my stomach that was telling me to run — run hard and fast. At that very moment it didn't matter what it was; everything was paid for. How could I call this off? I was not going to embarrass my mother or myself. She had worked overtime for over a year to help me pay for my fairy tale platinum wedding.

When I think back to that day, I was crying because I knew in my gut I was making a mistake. Being 25 years old I didn't have the strength or the heart to listen to my inner voice. Ella said to me that day what so many other people had said, "You are not the same at 25 years old as you will be at 30, and so forth." I was completely unaware of my reality. My reality was that "I, Grace, was lacking spirituality, maturity, and wisdom." Those are the tools you need to hear and listen to the voice of God. I chose to purse the fairy tale because I didn't have the strength and courage to walk away.

CHAPTER 3

Can I get this annulled?

On June 23, 2001, I married Mr. LC in a lavish wedding ceremony with over 200 people in attendance. The wedding was absolutely beautiful. We spared no expense. Each table centerpiece cost over $100, filled with roses flown in from Ecuador. We had a live band and DJ, open bar all night long. It was my perfect fairy tale wedding.

At the conclusion of a fairy tale wedding, most people expect the bride and groom to be swept away and begin their honeymoon. Well that was not how my wedding night went. My fairy tale wedding night went like this: I walked out of the catering hall with Mr. LC, along with my maid of honor, and got into her boyfriend's car. He was taking us home. Mr. LC left me in our friend's car and went to walk one of his brothers to another car. Well he left me waiting for well over twenty minutes. I became enraged. I felt like, "*This is our wedding night; take care of me! I am now your wife.*" Not to mention, I had an insane amount of Jack Daniels and champagne in my system. Mr. LC got back in the car; I did what any self-respecting bridezilla would have done; I took my tiara off my head and began to hit him with it. Oh wait, it gets better.

It did not stop there. I demanded to be taken to my mother's house. I don't know how, but somehow about three of my bridesmaids came along for "the show." There I was in my wedding gown, in a drunken stupor, asking, "Can I just this annulled?" In the midst of this craziness, I was also concerned as to whether or not I was going to be able to give Mr. LC children. I was drunk and delirious.

My mother had finally had enough of my shenanigans and kicked Karee (my maid of honor) and me out of her house. The final straw for my mother was when Karee tried to finagle her way to Hawaii, aka my honeymoon. So needless to say, I spent my wedding night with Karee. The next morning I fell out of her bed. Then her mother said, "Come on." I said, "Where are you taking me?" She answered, "Home; you're married now." I must have still been drunk. Otherwise, had I been sober, I would have run away.

Talk about a walk of shame. I got dropped off to our apartment. Mr. LC was waiting for me at the door. He said he "cried all night," which I never believed. After having what is commonly known as "make-up sex," we headed to Hawaii for twelve days of sun, sex, and more Jack Daniels.

Hawaii was paradise. In Hawaii, all was right in the world. I decided that I actually wanted to be married to this guy. I figured that's what marriage was — the good, the bad, and the ugly.

We came back from our honeymoon. Everyone chalked up my wedding night fiasco to "that was Gracie, being a spoiled prima donna," and "too much alcohol." We all went along as if it never even happened. It was a family secret. I mean I did not want anyone to know that I didn't spend my wedding night with my husband.

I was ready to move on with my happily ever after. My euphoria didn't last long. Shortly after we returned from Hawaii, Mr. LC, my mother, and I were all shopping in Target. That's when I got the call from my ob-gyn, who said that my pap smear had come back abnormal again. All I could think was, "*Is this really happening?*"

Now about a year prior to this I had been diagnosed with HPV (Human Papillomavirus). Mr. LC was by my side the entire time. Every doctor's visit, every procedure, which was one of the major reasons I thought he was such a great guy and future husband. My mother was a nurse; she thought it was time to find an oncologist. She suggested that I have a baby while I was young and said she would help us with whatever we needed for the baby. But was I ready for a baby? Absolutely not, or better yet, hell no!

So you can imagine, I was 25 years old and just married. Decided I actually loved Mr. LC and was feeling scared I wasn't going to be able to have children. All I could think was that I was going to die from cervical cancer. All this stress led me into a minor depression. This was not a part of the fairy tale. As we all do, I asked God, "*Why me?*" I had known girls who had slept with two dozen more men, and they didn't have HPV. I felt sorry for myself and was mentally preparing for the worst.

My mother found two amazing doctors who assured me that I was young and healthy, and if treated correctly, the HPV would not progress to cancer. Additionally, I would have no problems conceiving children. I scheduled a minor procedure and waited to heal. With my mother's and doctors' prompting, I got off my birth control pills. I was told it would take about a year for the pill to get out of my system. So Mr. LC and I went on living life and traveling, of course.

On top of the stress of my health, things were really difficult on the marriage front. It was more than just the typical growing and learning pains of living with someone. I had never lived with a man before. My mother taught me, "Why buy the cow when you can have the milk for free?" She came from that generation of "doing it the right way":

ring, marriage, baby carriage. So, it was a major adjustment for me, to say the least. Mr. LC was putting his family and their needs before me. He had no concept of what marriage meant. It is God's order, "For this reason a man shall leave his father and mother and be joined to his wife, and the two shall become one flesh" (Ephesians 5:31). It was impossible for us to grow together as man and wife when I was number five on his priority list. I told him repeatedly, "It's your grandmother, your mother, your aunt, your son, and then your wife."

I was resentful of his lying about how much money he actually made and the amount of debt he had. We argued about money, his family, and his priorities. I started looking into MBA programs. I had a stressful corporate job but made excellent money. I had to weigh the pros and cons of maybe taking a lower-paying job to focus on graduate school. Not working was not an option. We had household bills and were saving for a house.

As I look back, we were never on the same page about lifestyles and goals. It was all just bullshit to get me.

CHAPTER 4

"I think you've made a mistake – I'm not pregnant"

There are days that forever change your life and your schema of the world. That day for me, as for many Americans, was September 11, 2001. I was headed into New York City for a job interview that day and afterward meeting a friend for lunch. My friend's partner was a travel agent, and the interview was for a job as a travel consultant. She thought that would be a perfect fit for me while I went back to school. The job itself would have been less demanding than my corporate job. I was scheduled to take the train into the World Trade Center for the interview. But as God would have it I was running late that day, which meant I had to drive in. As I was getting dressed, my phone rang; my friend Ella was frantic. She said, "Where are you?" I said, "Home, walking out the door for the city." She said, "Gracie, turn on the news. You can't go into the city, there's been explosions."

I turned on the television. I saw the second tower come down. I dropped to my knees and started crying. Had I been on time I would have been at the World Trade Center during the attack. I immediately called Mr. LC to tell him to come home from work. No one knew what was going to become of those horrific attacks. Our first thought was to stock up on water and food. I also called the friend whom I was meeting for lunch to make sure she was safe. She was headed back to the Bronx. It was an extremely scary and uncertain time. I felt safe, knowing I had my husband to comfort and protect me. As the truth unfolded about the terrorist attacks on 9/11 as well as the realization of how many people lost parents, children, husbands, and wives, we were devastated by the senseless loss of lives. We considered ourselves blessed to have each other. Mr. LC and I talked all night about how there is nothing more important than family. We agreed that we definitely wanted to start our family next year.

Every year our family tried to take a vacation together. We were a bit uneasy because of what had occurred on 9/11. The reality was security was at an all-time high. It was probably the safest time to travel. In October of 2001, my mother, brother, grandmother, my girl TJ, Mr. LC, and I took a Caribbean cruise. Mr. LC and I did what we did best: ate, drank, had fun! Now if you have ever been on a cruise you know the food is non-stop. I was eating like it was going out of style. During the entire cruise after stuffing myself, I rubbed my stomach and joked that I had "little baby Dylan" in my belly. I laughed so hard, because in my mind, I couldn't get pregnant for at least a year. My mother called me a little piglet. Those were good times!

Well, we came back from the cruise and all was going well. I had started working at the travel agency and looking into graduate school programs. A month or so later I started not to feel so well. My boobs started hurting and my stomach was just really funky. It was time for my six-month ob-gyn follow-up appointment. Please read this: It does not take a year for birth control to get out of your system! On December 4, 2001, my doctor told me that I was pregnant. Of course I knew more than the doctor, so I responded, "You've made a mistake; I can't be pregnant." She laughed and said, "Why can't you?" I'm not sure of my exact comeback, but I'm sure it was witty. Nevertheless, I left the office with a black and white, completely unreadable picture of my little bambino. I remember two things after the appointment. First, riding home in complete and utter shock. Second, telling Mr. LC that no one will come before this child. In other words, *It's time for you to man up and get your shit together.*

What I meant by that is the fact that he promised me that once we were married he was going to sell the two-family home that his family lived in to his parents. That way his credit would be free to buy a home for us. Here I was unexpectedly pregnant and living in a three-bedroom apartment in Union, New Jersey. Our rent was the same amount as a mortgage payment. At the time, we needed a bedroom for his son. I was really anxious about how we were going to be able to afford to buy a house with our credit card debt. We decided to move into a smaller, one-bedroom apartment so we could pay down debt, save money, and buy our house. I always knew in the back of my mind, he was never going to sell that house. His family had made him the "golden child savior" and he was not going to disappoint them. They were always his first priority.

I had to just focus on my unborn baby and what I could control. I chose not to stress over the house not being for sale or any of his other lies. I was beyond excited for my baby. I had enjoyed a wonderful pregnancy with no complications. On July 30, 2002, one year after our wedding anniversary, I gave birth to our daughter, Sarah Carrington. She was a blessing and all that was perfect in the world. She changed my life forever. I experienced a love that cannot be expressed. It was my life's duty to protect, love, spoil, and nurture her.

Another powerful moment in my life was when Sarah was 6 weeks old, and we took our family vacation to Cape

Cod. My mother, nephew, cousin, Mr. LC's son, Mr. LC, and I took the drive from New Jersey. It was probably the worst vacation I had ever experienced.

My relationship with Mr. LC's son was strained since before I had married his father. This was a child who had never even been to summer camp until I came into the picture. I never tried to be his mother; that was not my place. But his behavior was truly disrespectful. At the time he was 8 years old and had no manners. He was caught telling lies to both parents, both of whom I blame: his mother, because she would undermine Mr. LC's attempts to provide structure and discipline, and Mr. LC, who felt guilty that his son was not living with him full time.

The Sunday after we got back home from Cape Cod, I went to church. I remember feeling so overwhelmed with the joy of having my daughter. However, I also knew that I needed Jesus to give me patience to deal with Mr. LC's son. It became clear that I needed the power of God to get me through this journey called life and motherhood. It was at that Sunday service I went to the altar, joined the church, and decided I wanted to be baptized. In addition to needing God in my life, I wanted my children to grow up in the church.

Four months later, on January 15, 2003, I was baptized at New Hope Baptist Church in East Orange, New Jersey. I was baptized by the same pastor who married Mr. LC and me, just a short year and a half ago. I never thought that I would grow as deep as I did with God. I was happy, knew that I loved the Lord, but was not completely sold out for Christ. I still wanted to do things my way.

CHAPTER 5

Another sucker punch

I was so happy with my angel, Sarah. Everything was about her and her future. As most parents do, I wanted the very best for her always. A part of that included her growing up in a home with a backyard in a safe community with excellent schools. That was my goal. We worked hard to make that a reality for her and ourselves.

What Mr. LC managed to do over and over again during our marriage was "sucker punch" me in the stomach when it was least expected. In other words, he would do something that pulled the rug from right underneath me. I did not realize it then, but he never had any respect or consideration for my feelings. Let me give a very clear example of what I mean: It was the spring of 2003 and we were preparing to meet with the mortgage broker to pre-qualify for our mortgage. I distinctly remember asking Mr. LC, "Is there anything I should know about before we go?" His response was no. I was elated to finally be able to start house hunting. We happily took the ride down to South Jersey to meet with our broker. As we sat there with the broker, the "punch" came. The broker said to Mr. LC, "You have been late on your current mortgage several times." I instantly felt a knot in my stomach, and I just looked at Mr. LC. I was so embarrassed and thought to myself, "*What in the hell is his problem? I just asked him if there was anything I should know?*" The ride home was very tense. He gave some pathetic excuse, "Oh, I didn't think it was going to show up." Trust is the foundation of every relationship, and without trust you have nothing. Every time something like that happened I lost more and more respect for Mr. LC.

Despite his less than stellar credit score, we were able to get approved for our mortgage. We purchased and closed on our first home. It was all good! We achieved the American Dream: home ownership. It was a beautiful three-bedroom center hall colonial in South Orange, New Jersey. I was in awe that I had my very own home. I was all caught up in the excitement of decorating and hosting parties. My fairy tale was shaping up quite nicely.

As the years passed, everything was about Sarah, and giving her everything I never had. Wanting more for her than I had myself. I was still working at the travel agency; he was still working for an insurance company. We were traveling, having dinner parties... life was good. I was so madly in love with the illusion of my life. From the outside everything was perfect. However, inside the marriage I was very lonely.

Mr. LC had started actively pursuing opening up a bar with his then-best friend — one of the shadiest people I know. His business partner, "Mr. BS," was a man who would brag about flying other women into New Jersey. Mr. BS would wine and dine his mistresses and repeatedly threaten his wife by saying he would sell their family house. I asked Mr. LC how could he trust Mr. BS? Mr. LC assured me that Mr. BS's personal business had nothing to do with their friendship and business. I was left alone a lot and felt empty. What better way to fill the void of an unsatisfying marriage than to have more children, of course! Seriously, I wanted two more children at the time. I thought that if I had my children, my life would be more complete and I would look less toward the marriage to make me happy.

We started trying to have another baby. It didn't take long before I was pregnant again. I was so excited, and since my pregnancy with Sarah was perfect I didn't feel the need to wait the recommended twelve weeks to share the good news with our family and friends. We told everyone. But happiness with Mr. LC never lasted long. I remember like it was yesterday: I was driving down Parker Street in Maplewood, New Jersey. Mr. LC called me saying that his car had gotten broken into at his brother's house in East Orange. He had our toddler with him during this fiasco. I started cursing and screaming at him and said, "I can't understand why you continue to take my daughter to the ghetto! That's why we moved away from that environment. Bring my daughter back home now!" I hung up the phone on him. I was so upset that I was shaking. He brought Sarah home and apologized. I was still furious and gave him the silent treatment. That was a regular occurrence in our house if he did something I did not like.

He had always made really poor choices. For example after I had just given birth to Sarah, Mr. LC wanted his father to meet her. He brought his father, who was high on drugs, to our tiny apartment. My mother was there (helping me with the baby) and she couldn't believe that he would bring his father in that state around a new baby. That night I cried myself to sleep, because I knew this man would never put me and/or our children first.

Shortly after Mr. LC's car incident in East Orange, we went to Jamaica for vacation in February 2004. While there I started spotting. My mother was with us and she said that it was probably just first trimester spotting. In my heart I knew that something was wrong. I was an emotional wreck during the vacation. I wasn't home more than a week when I started bleeding again. This time, I was at work. I called my doctor, and she told me to go to the hospital. Mr. LC picked me up from work and we went to the hospital. My doctor was not available, so I waited in the emergency room for about an hour. I had blood work and an ultrasound done. After waiting for the results for what seemed like forever, I was told by some unsympathetic ER doctor, "There is no baby." My heart stopped and I was void of any emotion. I don't remember the car ride home or whether I cried that night. However, I cried non-stop for the next three to four weeks. It was awful.

To make matters worse, I had to wait three days to have the DNC procedure with my doctor. I had whatever remained of my child, whom I will always call "Jonah," in my womb, until I could be "cleaned out." My heart was so heavy. I was not allowed to grieve. I had my family telling me, "Be grateful that you have Sarah," "That's God's way of taking care of things," or "God doesn't give you more than you can bare" — all the things people say all the time. They mean well, but it doesn't take away from the hurt and pain. Miscarriage is a pain that can't quite be put into words. When a woman who wants a baby finds out she is pregnant it's in that very moment she is carrying her child, not an embryo — a baby. It was especially devastating for me because children were my source of joy.

In Mr. LC's attempt to make me happy, he said we could take a trip anywhere I wanted to go. I decided that we would go to St. Barts. St. Barts was so beautiful, serene, chic, and romantic. The island also had the most amazing cuisine. I was able to clear my mind, relax, and come to terms with my loss. I was able to find joy again. As always, the vacation was enough to make me fall back in love with my husband and my fairy tale life. I felt sexy again, surrounded by all the other beautiful people. I was able to be romantic with Mr.

LC. St. Barts was absolutely amazing! It will always be one of my favorite destinations.

After we returned home from vacation, I was told I had to wait three months before I could try to conceive again. It was the longest three months of my life. So I kept myself busy, and Mr. LC was becoming more and more distant. I was disgusted with him coming home late and his lies. All I cared about was getting pregnant again. One night while on the phone with my mother I was feeling extremely emotional and hormonal. Enough time had passed that Mr. LC and I had started to try to have another baby, but I honestly did not think that I was pregnant.

I hung up with my mother, went upstairs, and took a pregnancy test. I had several in stock. I peed on the stick and sure enough I was pregnant. How many women do you know find out they are pregnant and do not even bother to call their husbands? I called my mother back and told her the good news. Then I cried myself to sleep, because I knew my husband was out with some whore. He came home at his usual 3 o' clock in the morning. He made his infamous pit stop to the bathroom (a man's pitiful attempt to clean himself before coming to bed). He came in our bedroom and said, "What is this?" I said, "What do you think it is?" I rolled over and went back to sleep.

During that time, I kept wondering, "*Is this what marriage is? I have the security of a husband, a home, cars, a child, and expensive gifts. How can I complain? Maybe this is what love looks like.*" Either way, I couldn't focus on Mr. LC. I needed to put my love, energy, and attention on making sure I had a healthy baby.

CHAPTER 6

The beginning of the end: bar, booze, and bitches

Although I was so grateful to be pregnant, it was a very difficult pregnancy with my second daughter. I started bleeding in my second trimester. Since I had miscarried before, my doctor put me on bed rest just to be safe. I hurt everywhere — my back, my ass, my stomach — it was just awful. I was also still working. However, we had agreed that after I had the second baby I would stay home for at least a year or two. Oh yeah, this is the fairy tale life: a provider husband, being home to take care of the kids, and spending afternoons at the mall with play dates to occupy your days. I took pride in being a wife and a mother. Mr. LC came home to cooked meals every day. I made sure the house was clean and the laundry was done, and I never denied my husband sex. An old Italian woman told me before I got married, "Whenever your husband's hungry, make sure you cook the macaroni." Basically, never deny your husband sex, otherwise someone else will gladly "feed him." (That didn't matter to Mr. LC; he still ate at other places even with me "cooking the macaroni" at home.) I struggled internally: On one hand this was what I wanted, and on the other I was so miserable. This really wasn't the life I envisioned for myself. I began to wonder, how did I get caught up in this lifestyle?

During this very difficult pregnancy, I needed Mr. LC, but he wasn't there. He had started in the bar business, while still working his corporate job. Mr. LC was always working. Now, probably the biggest lie Mr. LC told me was that they (he and Mr. BS) were not going to operate the bar. They would rent the bar space out to someone who had a liquor license and collect the rent from the six apartments on top of the bar. It's funny how once you realize that you have been lied to from the very beginning; you start to become angry with yourself. I was angry because I believed his lies.

Anyhow, I was told that two potential people who previously had their liquor licenses fell through as renters for the bar. Their "only option" was to buy a license and operate the bar themselves. So Mr. LC and Mr. BS ended up buying a license from another bar in Hillside. The plan was to operate at the Hillside location for a couple of months and then transfer it to the Vice Lounge. The Vice Lounge was located in the building they purchased, with the six apartments on top of the bar. So it all continued on a larger scale, the late nights and never-ending stories of lies, and of course, the string of women.

In the midst of all of this, on April 18, 2005, I gave birth to Victoria Carrington. She was so big in my belly they thought I was having twins. We also did not find out the sex of the baby until I was seven months pregnant. She had her legs closed every time we went for an ultrasound. She was a big beautiful baby, with a head full of hair. In true fairy tale fashion, I had a vacation planned for exactly six weeks after I had given birth to Victoria. We went to Puerto Rico. Here we go again, one big happy family (on the outside). I wrote Mr. LC a five-page letter. I poured my heart out. I asked Mr. LC to talk to me, to go to therapy, couples counseling — anything to save our marriage. He read it and cried. He agreed to go to counseling together. Even though I was so unhappy at the time, I still wanted my marriage to work.

I never saw myself getting a divorce at that point. I still loved him and my fairy tale very much. More important, I wanted my girls to grow up with both of their parents. I had never failed at anything and I wasn't going to fail at my family. I didn't have my father in my life for over ten years. I didn't want my girls to ever experience those feelings of separation, abandonment or feel like they came from a "broken home." So, I made it my business to keep my family together, even at the cost of my happiness.

Victoria had been a very fussy baby, crying all the time. We took her to the doctor and nothing was wrong. It was overwhelming. I was finally able to stay home and I was miserable. There was nothing to comfort her or me for that matter. Two months after having Victoria, I remember rocking my newborn baby girl and crying on the phone. It was my fourth wedding anniversary and I did not want to go out or celebrate with Mr. LC. Everyone said I was just hormonal because I had just had the baby.

Mr. LC had reservations for dinner at the Chart House. My tits were still swollen and I felt like I weighed a thousand pounds. We went out and I told myself, "*He loves you, you're his wife.*" Mr. LC said all the right things at dinner. We went home, we made love, and there we were again in that sick, vicious cycle. Another year went by and I was happy. I had my two beautiful daughters, my house, my car, my vacations, and my jewelry. What more could I ask for? My husband was a part of my fairy tale as well. However, he had other "interests" that kept him detached.

I focused on what I did best, which was being a good mother and wife and maintaining our home. I had established a routine for the house that worked for our family. One day, I had a curve ball thrown my way. Mr. LC's best friend, Mr.

BS, brought him home. I asked, "What happened to your company car, why are you home early?" Then I heard the words that no wife wants to hear. Mr. LC said, "They let me go." On the outside I was cool, calm, and collected. On the inside I was like, "*Oh my freaking god! What are we going to do?*" I couldn't even ask before Mr. LC reassured me that the "bar will make enough money to take care of everything."

I thought, "*Is he smoking crack? We have a mortgage, two small kids, one kid in private school, car notes, I'm on my way back to graduate school*" — the list went on and on. Once again, I played the good wife. I smiled, agreed with him, and said, "We will all be all right."

Being laid off from his insurance job gave him even more time to pursue his other interests. As a result of him working full time at the bar, he increased the number of late nights during the week. I could not say a word, because at that point it was the source of all the income coming into the home.

Chapter 7

I need you to come home!

Through my personal life experience, I have learned that what some men do when they are cheating is give us things. They rationalize that their affairs have nothing to do with their love for their partner. On the surface, these gifts are to prove "how much they love us." Sadly all those "gifts" are just distractions. I have a funny little story to demonstrate this point. It's called the "Where's my Camry?" story.

Now, we always leased cars. When Mr. LC was laid off he lost his company car. Therefore, we needed another car. He was full time at the bar and I had my mommy duties. I figured, "*OK, let's be practical.*" I already had a truck, and I suggested, "Let's just get the Toyota Camry." We went to at least two different dealers, maybe even three. I got so fed up with the slime ball car dealers, I told Mr. LC, "I'm keeping my truck, go get yourself a car. I'll drive your car when you need the truck for the bar on your liquor runs and the restaurant depot."

He went out, test drove the 750 BMW, and then a Benz. He called me and said that he picked out his car and we had to go pick it up at the dealer. With my two bambinos in tow, we headed to Ray Catena Mercedes Benz to pick up daddy's car. Once I arrived, it was like people were expecting me — another one of Mr. LC's unforgettable moments. This was a scene that was a perfect fit in my fairy tale life. The sales rep said, "Oh Mrs. Carrington, your husband picked you out a beautiful car." I looked at Mr. LC and smiled. Well,

well, to my surprise my wonderful husband had picked out a brand new 2006 C280 4MATIC. It was beautiful; black with beige interior. All I could do was shake my head. Now I know most of you are thinking, *Wow, that was an upgrade from a Camry!*

However, there are two very important lessons to this story: 1. The Mercedes was not so much for me, but more for Mr. LC's ego, so he could hear over and over, "LC bought Gracie another Benz." Let's not forget — he told everyone he bought my first Mercedes. 2. If he really wanted to give me what I wanted he would have brought home a damn Camry, with more back leg room! Nevertheless, I drove it off the lot. Of course I did; it went right along with my fairy tale. With two small kids and strollers, I preferred the Durango, but who was I to complain? People would have thought I was obnoxious.

So now here comes the part of the story that gets really juicy; stay with me. It was August 2006, eight days before I was to start graduate school. Mr. LC was at the Vice lounge working. I was home like the good wife, talking on the phone to my girl Karee. I opened our bank statement and to my surprise, there was $60,000 missing from our account. I don't even remember what I said to Karee, but I hung up and called Mr. LC.

I said, "Honey, I need you to come home, now." He said, "I can't, I'm busy working." I said, "There's money missing from our account." "I know," he said. In complete panic, I said, "No, a lot of money!" Then Mr. LC casually told me that he gave it to his business partner to open up his other bar. I completely lost it. I yelled and screamed and told him to bring his ass home now! I was in shock and disbelief, pacing the floor. I had two babies upstairs sleeping, but I needed answers immediately. At one point I thought," *Is he leaving me? But why would he buy me a new car just to leave me?"* I was a mess, a complete mess.

He came through the door, and tried to act all tough like he was a damn rapper or somebody. He told me, "It's my money," since the money was from the proceeds from the sale of his two-family house in Newark. We argued and I kicked him out. I told him he had to put the money back by the next day. I woke up the next day, threw on some clothes, and took out the remainder of what was in the account, roughly $30,000. I was still in shock, I had been crying all night, and the girls were asking for their father. I went to my bank, opened up a money market account and waited to hear answers from this man.

I reached out to my father to talk to him about everything that happened. I asked him to talk to Mr. LC and get answers. Of course Mr. LC poured out more lies to my father. He promised never to lie to me again. (Remember this, because the following five years are going to be filled with lie after lie.)

I called the people closest to me and got their advice. I was actually considering whether or not to hold off starting graduate school. I was beside myself.

A couple of days later, Mr. LC came to the house. We went to TGI Fridays in West Orange to talk. Basically, he told me that he lied about how much money was made from the sale of the Newark house. He stated that all that was missing was $20,000. He said he gave $10,000 to his business partner, $5,000 for house bills, and another $5,000 down on my Mercedes. In other words, the money was not coming back. None of the story made sense. I honestly did not know what to believe. I had seen the bank account with my own eyes. How does that amount of money just disappear?

Once again, it really didn't matter — I had bigger fish to fry. I was starting my graduate program in five days. After my family's insistence, I agreed to let Mr. LC back in the house. Honestly, I needed him to pay the bills. I knew that if I kept him out he would have shacked up with one of his whores. I'm no fool. So I put on my game face, pretended to forgive him, and decided to keep it moving. I secretly declared to myself, "*Fuck him, I'm going to do me.*" Not in the sense that I was going to cheat, but I if wanted to go out and have fun I would. No more sitting at home like the good wife. After that stunt he pulled with the money, coupled with his cheating, it was no longer if I would get divorced, but rather when.

At the time I had it all planned out: I would stay married until Sarah went to college and then leave. Sadly, I was still trying to plan my life even as it was falling apart right before my eyes. Things got worse for me whenever I would think about having to stay with him for that long. I started having panic attacks. I would cry and ponder what would happen to me. Am I going to be able to raise two small children, do well in grad school, take care of a house, and deal with his bullshit?

I had always been good at pretending to be happy. This time was different; I could not pretend. I was not happy and I really wanted to divorce him right then. That was not an option because I was jobless, starting school, and afraid what it would do to the girls. So, at the recommendation of a friend, I thought about starting therapy to deal with all the drama and deceit.

CHAPTER 8

I can do it better

I started a master of social work program. It was a two-year full-time program with clinical work as well as course work. I was excited, nervous, and mentally wiped out. I knew I needed to complete grad school to be able to provide for my daughters. (Which would later prove to be the case.) I started school the very same day my baby Sarah started pre-K at St. Joseph's in Maplewood. It was so cute.

I had decided that I really needed to go to counseling to deal with this failing marriage. The therapist had her own agenda. Her agenda was to save my marriage. That is not want I needed. I needed to figure out how I ended up in this mess and how I really felt about the marriage. As a therapist, you have to respect your client's right to self-determination. I was able to express some of my feelings, but I felt judged. Mr. LC even went with me to a session or two. He put on the performance of a lifetime; he even cried! I vaguely remember him saying that he "would do whatever it takes to save our marriage."

I remember sitting in that session so disgusted I could have vomited. I knew that it was all bullshit. Let's not forget, he was still coming home at 3 or 4 o'clock in the morning, when the bar closed at 2 a.m.

The money was rolling in and my fairy tale was now becoming to look like an episode of *Lifestyles of the Rich and Famous*. We took car service into the city for birthdays, three vacations a year, and I was a regular at Short Hills Mall. We would go to the most exclusive restaurants in the City. Mr. LC and his business partner would travel to the NBA All-Star weekends. The list goes on and on. It got to the point that I started not even to care what Mr. LC did.

I decided that I was going to start doing me. I said to myself, "*If he can do it, I can do it, and better!*" How better? I told him what I was doing. I decided that I wanted to be with women again. Yes, close your mouth, I said a woman. Prior to meeting and marrying Mr. LC, I had several relationships with women. I had considered myself bisexual in college. However, once I married my Prince Charming, I ditched all my pride for the fairy tale. Mr. LC had known about my history, but I had assured him that those thoughts and desires where no longer. Honestly, I hadn't thought about being with a woman the entire time we were married prior to all this drama. But at that point, I just needed a stress release, in the form of a hot, sexy love affair.

One night I went out with some friends to an infamous gay dive bar in Newark. I met this girl, and so it began. She was so pretty, and I'd had one drink too many. She asked me for my number and I said, "No, give me yours." I took her number, thinking to myself, "*I still have it.*" Still somewhat hungover I called her on my way to class the next day. We made plans to meet for dinner and we did. She was a little rough around the edges, but I didn't care. I just wanted to have fun. We actually had a lot of fun together. I felt she was a safe reintroduction into that "life" that I had left over six years ago.

Mr. LC knew about her. In fact he called her and invited her to our annual New Year's Eve party. Thank God, she declined the invite. It was that very night Mr. LC and I got into a huge argument. He had become insecure about my relationship with her, mostly because I no longer cared what time he came home. I had found someone who wanted to be with me. Honestly, we mostly watched movies and had dinners together. Funny enough, once he found out about "Betty," all of a sudden he was able to make his way home by 1:30 a.m. Pathetic. So on New Year's Eve of 2006, I emphatically told Mr. LC, "I can't promise you forever anymore." He started to cry. What did I care after all he had put me through? Not to mention, I had a party to host, which happened to be one of the best New Year's Eve parties we had ever had.

The fling with "Betty" was short-lived. However, I had found a new conquest. We will call her "Amanda." She was a classmate and seven years my junior. I am a Leo, and we love a conquest. She would be coy, demure, and by all accounts a "good girl." She even had a boyfriend. But what did that mean to me? I had a cheating, lying husband.

Our friendship took a turn on spring break in Miami circa 2007. I left my cheating husband and my two babies and went to Miami for the weekend with a good friend at the time. Amanda's close friend invited herself and Amanda's cousin on this trip. I didn't care, I had my own agenda to relax and get away from Mr. LC. So picture it: In some dark, hot Miami nightclub, I started dancing with Amanda. I said to her, "So tell me why your boyfriend isn't fucking you, because I would." She was speechless, and I half-regretted saying it. I was going to be like Jamie Foxx and "blame it on the alcohol." In my crazy mind, I thought, "*The fact that she didn't slap me meant one thing: Game on!*"

The next night we all went back out and she grabbed my hand. I jerked my hand away because her holier-than-thou cousin and friend were there. I didn't need them judging me. In my mind, I was completely justified in my actions. We left Miami and headed back to New Jersey and it started:

"the chase." For a Leo there is nothing is better and hotter than a good game of cat and mouse.

Now I have to push pause on this story to tell you what was going on back on the marriage ranch. As you can imagine, our marriage was just a façade at this point. The way I saw it, I was stuck there for the next ten years for the kids, he was still cheating, I was cheating, and the money was still coming in. So I'm feeling like, if it's not broke don't fix it. I know — completely insane, but at the time it just seemed normal. Or at least, my normal.

We decided to move to a bigger house. I wanted to move to a better school district for my kids. Private school was just way too expensive when you do the numbers for what it would cost to educate two kids from kindergarten through high school, so we began house hunting for a bigger home. Now pay attention: I had two small kids, was attending graduate program, buying a bigger house, selling my current home, and lastly, having an affair. Now for some of you this sounds familiar, because some of us will do anything to escape our reality. And as crazy as this sounds I was happy. I did not have to deal with a failing marriage. I had the security and comfort of being married to Mr. LC. When the opportunity presented itself, I had my moments and hours of happiness with Amanda.

Now back to Amanda — we would text back and forth and go for coffee, shopping, and out to dinners all in the name of "friends." I was "putting in work." All that changed on April 10, 2007. I motioned for her to lean in, she did, and the rest is history. It was an intense emotional roller coaster for the next four years. We could not stop even when I tried to pull away. I had stopped going to therapy. I didn't need it, I was happy.

In the summer of 2007 we moved to Green Brook, New Jersey. The buyer fell through for our house in South Orange. We had bought the new house not contingent upon the sale of our current home, so we had to take out a home equity loan on South Orange for $100,000 to put down on Green Brook. Mr. LC and I packed up our two daughters and moved up the hill to suburbia. It was my dream home. It featured four bedrooms, three bathrooms, a paver patio, and a stainless steel kitchen. It sat on over an acre of protected land. This would be the family home that our daughters would grow up in, according to my fairy tale. I envisioned their proms and their weddings pictures taken there. I later found out that Mr. LC told our neighbors, "We moved to have more children." Absolutely insane; the lies were never-ending. Maybe that was his fairy tale?

This fairy tale was always just in my mind and heart. Mr. LC and I were rarely on the same page. Here's a story to illustrate that fact. That summer I asked Mr. LC if we could send our oldest daughter to an amazing summer camp. I always wanted the very best for my girls. However, I will be the first to admit that the camp was expensive. This was not just some average camp; this was a state-of-the-art summer camp where the kids went swimming, did archery, horseback riding, rock climbing, and tons of other cool stuff. He told me it was too expensive and to find a cheaper camp. So I did as I was told, and it was fine.

However, not less than three weeks later he came home with a brand new 2007 Yukon Denali XL. Allow me to expand upon this for the folks who are not into cars and trucks. That truck was massive. The car note was $700 a month. Putting gas into that truck was a nightmare; $100 did not even get half a tank of gas. He made such poor choices. I was told that he works hard, he should get what he wants; he "deserved it." I am not saying that he didn't. Allow me to paint the full picture. I told Mr. LC, "You keep the Mercedes and I will get a used car, perhaps the Camry you never bought me." My rationale was that we just moved into this big house. We did not know how the winter was going to be with respect to gas, bills, snow removal, and overall maintenance. Not to mention that we had not sold the house in South Orange, we just had a tenant in there. I asked him to think about it, "*What if she stopped paying rent?*" He said, "Don't worry about money, it will be the company car and the bar will pay the car note." He called the Yukon the "White Stallion." I chalked it up to a mid-life crisis. All I could do was bite my tongue and pray it all worked out.

During the summer of 2007, I kept myself busy with trips to NYC, weekends down the shore, and baking, mostly with Amanda and, of course, my daughters. I put all my energy into taking care of my daughters, getting them ready for the new school, and adjusting to a new neighborhood. After settling into the new home and telling myself and everyone around me, "I'm happy". It started to fall apart less than four months after moving to Green Brook.

There was nothing in any of my psychology books that could have prepared me for the very real and hard life lessons that only God was about to teach me.

Chapter 9

"I didn't want to upset you"

We were now in the fall of 2007 and all was well. Mr. LC and I were sitting at home watching television. We got a call from one of our neighbors in South Orange. She said, *"Oh you didn't tell me that your tenant was moving out."* I said, "She's not." My neighbor responded, "Well there's a moving truck in front of your house." Mr. LC jumped up and went to the house in South Orange. Now before this point, she had been late a couple times and her security check bounced, but she made good on it. Mr. LC handled that entire situation, and as you can see it was a fiasco. He just went with the first person. When he got to South Orange, the tenant had this long, crazy story of how she had to move because her ex-husband found out where she was living. To make a long story short, Mr. LC ended up taking her to court and getting a $10,000 judgment against her. The only problem is that a person has to have assets, money, and/or come into some money, in order for the judgment to really mean anything. It's like that old saying; "You can't get blood from a rock."

We were paying mortgages for both homes, which totaled $5,000 a month. The house in South Orange was vacant. We still had other bills that included health insurance, childcare, utilities, car insurances, gas, my Mercedes car note, and the $700 Yukon Denali car note. I was beginning to panic. I still had another year of graduate school, which meant I could not work until I finished.

Thanksgiving of 2007, we received a notice from the bank about the South Orange house that stated we were not making the payments. I asked Mr. LC what was going on? He swore he was making the payments, but they were late.

My mother decided she was going to move into our house in South Orange. She said she was doing this so there wouldn't be "a strain on the marriage." I just started crying to her and told her about the bank notice. (Now it's important to mention, I had never told her about the stunt he pulled taking the $60,000 out of our account.) She said not to worry about it, it would all work out. So she moved in and paid us a good portion, but we still had to add to the payment in order to make the mortgage. I was grateful, because that meant we didn't have to pay two mortgages. This was when the market had crashed and it was a tough housing market.

Not less than a month later in December 2007, Mr. LC lost his partnership in the bar. My fairy tale was becoming a nightmare.

Mr. LC came home one night and said that he was "leaving the bar." I was in complete shock. My mind was racing — *"How the hell are we going to survive?"* I remained calm enough to hear his convoluted, bullshit story. He said that his partner, Mr. BS, accused him of stealing money. Then my husband had the nerve to say that he was "tired of living that lifestyle," I said to myself, "*I guess drinking and staying out till 3 a.m. with your whore was getting to become too much for you.*"

Mr. LC said that he was going to be bought out of the business by Mr. BS.

He carried on and on about how Mr. BS said that *"I was going to leave him after I graduated from grad school."* Along with the accusation that Mr. LC stole money from the bar to buy our house, which was a complete lie. Honestly, I did raise my eyebrow at the accusation of him stealing money, because Mr. LC had proven over and over to me that he could not be trusted with money. (Now, I'm going all the way back to him mailing my bills late before we were even married.) He said that it was going to be a very simple business transaction. All that needed to be done was to transfer the liquor license to his partner's name. Mr. LC said he was going to the attorney's office that week to get a $50,000 check. The entire transaction would be complete in two to three months max. The payoff balance was going to be somewhere in the neighborhood of $120,000, then an additional $50,000 "on the back end." I begged him to get a lawyer to protect us; I said, "Think about the girls." I even called a good friend to see if she would represent him. He insisted he did not want to have to "waste money" on an attorney. My head was spinning.

Mr. LC assured me that it would be more than enough money to get us through me finishing school. He promised he was going to go back to working a regular 9 to 5 job. To make matters worse, in the midst of all of this I finally found proof of whom he was cheating with. It was one of the barmaids. I checked his phone, and of course he denied it. I couldn't help but think to myself, "*You threw away your marriage and family for a sloppy, trashy barmaid?*" I mean let's be honest: It's one thing when your husband cheats with the younger, sexier chick, but when it's a slut that half the world has run through, you don't get a pass. At this point, I was like, "*Fuck you and your whore. You two sorry people deserve each other. I have to take care of my girls!*"

So I brought in the year 2008 in church, asking God for a miracle. I wanted to leave Mr. LC and be with my lover. I was in the last semester of my graduate program. I had to focus on school and passing my license exam so I could get a job and support my kids. During this time, Mr. LC had yet to look for one job. He told me how difficult it was to go back to working for someone else after being his own boss. He wanted to use our savings, instead of looking for jobs. We were living off our credit cards and going broke.

I began to struggle with sleeping. I had so much stress, anxiety, and fear. "*How will I pay my mortgage when the money runs out? What if he never finds a job?*" I had the weight of the world on my shoulders. On the outside I was still smiling, pretending that I had it all under control. Every night Mr. LC lay in bed and slept like a baby. I, on the other hand, could not sleep. When I did sleep I had nightmares. I cried every night after I put my girls to bed. In his mind, it was all going to be done in a couple of months once he got that check for $120,000. I thought to myself, "*Is he delusional or psychotic?*" I would later find out he was both.

Chapter 10

Please don't let that be the mailman

It was crunch time at school. I was looking for jobs, studying for my license exam, and trying to hold it all together. Mr. LC decided he was going to start substitute teaching in the district where our daughters went to school. He was subbing just about every day, making about $85 a day. He also got a part-time job at Talbots in the mall. All this is a far cry from the $3,000 to $4,000 he used to bring home in a week. With all this going on, he was still having his affair with the barmaid. Oh I forgot to mention that she was fired too. Mr. BS fired her because she was allegedly helping Mr. LC steal the money. Shortly after Mr. LC's ability to take care of her was over, Ms. Barmaid was suddenly no longer interested in Mr. LC or calling him at all hours of the night.

I think one of my favorite moments during this Greek tragedy was when we were laying in bed one night. The repo men were outside coming for his beloved Denali, the White Stallion. He was sleeping like a baby. I had to wake him up so he could get the girls' car seats out of the truck. Oh yes, he still thought he could keep that truck. On his current salary, which was about $425 a week. It always reminds me of that comedy sketch from Chris Rock, when he says, "Look at them rims, N****. They spinning, they spinning." It was just so absurd. Not even ghetto-fabulous, just absolutely insane. I laugh even to this day, because in his sick mind a truck was more important than sowing seeds into his daughters' future.

By the grace of God, I made it through my master's program with honors. Even with all the stress of my personal life. I took my licensing exam on May 23, 2008, and I passed. I was excited and on my way home to celebrate with Amanda. She was baking a cake with my daughters and things were looking up for me. I got home and not even thirty minutes later the doorbell rang. It was the mailman. The letters were certified mail, all from Bank of America. I opened the letters and they were "notices for the intent to foreclose." I went upstairs to my room and I called the bank. I was confused — we were paying the mortgages? My mother was living in the South Orange house… what was going on? Well, nothing could have prepared me for what I was told. Mr. LC had not paid either mortgage in three months. I started crying hysterically. I jotted down dates of last payments and I was baffled. The money was not in our bank account. He was paying the mortgages online, is what he told me.

I called Mr. LC crying, saying, "What have you done?" He asked if he could come home to explain everything. I told him, "No, hell no." I did not trust him around the kids or me. In true Lifetime movie fashion, I packed a suitcase for my daughters and myself. We went to stay at Amanda's house. I never even got the chance to celebrate all my accomplishments. I was bombarded with all this drama, lies, and financial hardship. I stayed a night or two at Amanda's house. However, my father told me to go back to my house and kick Mr. LC out. I had been at this same place so many times before where I had kicked him out. That's exactly what I did for about two weeks.

At this point, I'm sure you want to know what did Mr. LC do with the mortgage money? I am going to tell you exactly what he told me: "I used it to pay bills." I asked, "What bill is more important than paying the bill for the roof over your children's heads?" Then he claimed he was "robbing Peter to pay Paul." At this point it did not matter. It didn't matter where the first $60,000 went; it didn't matter where this last $15,000 went. It was all gone, and never going to be replaced. I knew right then in that very moment that I was married to a very sick, emotionally disturbed, pathological liar. I had to get myself and my daughters away from him ASAP.

Chapter 11

Living with the enemy

One thing you should know about me is that I am a very methodical person. As much as I wanted to kick him out of the house permanently right after all this happened, I couldn't. It wasn't that simple. I was still unemployed; I had to think about the girls and paying my bills. I couldn't guarantee that he would do what I needed him to do if he moved out. So I had to do one of the hardest things I ever had to do in my life: I had to co-habit with this crazy, untrustworthy bastard, aka my husband. However, I made it very clear to him that we were getting a divorce. Him not paying our mortgages was absolutely the last straw.

Not many people knew we were separated and getting a divorce, so we pretended to still be together. Amanda and I were still together, but she was more of a great friend in the midst of all this chaos. She would give me scriptures to read and tell me I was strong enough to survive this. I did not want a lot of people in my personal business. After all, I spent years creating my fairy tale. It was hard enough dealing with the loss of my fairy tale life and living in this nightmare. I had a plan and I had to execute that plan:

1. Get a good job.
2. Stack my chips, aka save money.
3. Slowly introduce the every other weekend concept to my kids.
4. File bankruptcy.

5. Get a divorce.
6. Move to California.

In June of 2008, I had landed a great job working for a New Jersey Public School district. That was the first step, landing a well-paying job after grad school.

My daughters began to feel and question things regarding their father and me. Mr. LC moved into the third bedroom and when the kids asked, "Why is daddy sleeping in the other bedroom?" I would say, "Because mommy's back hurts." They asked a couple of times, and then they just got used to the idea. My oldest daughter completely witnessed the alienation of affection between her father and I. By this point I could not stand the sight of him, let alone him touching me. I would often give in to what we as woman call "sympathy sex." It's when you feel so bad for the poor bastard that you give in, but you hate it, fake it, and jump in the shower the minute it's over.

We managed to make it through the year co-habiting. I even started to question whether or not I should have him move out. We were like two ships passing in the night. When he came home, I walked out and vice versa. That would all change on May 17, 2009. It was the night before my breast reduction. Yes, in the midst of all this chaos, I decided to get my boobs done. (I wanted it done for me, not to get another man.) He had come in the house from allegedly working late.

Amanda was there with the girls and me. I do not remember the details. We started to argue and one thing led to another and I was chasing after him. I wanted him out of my house. We were screaming at each other and the girls heard us. They started to cry; it was the worst moment of my life. I knew instantly he had to go. I didn't feel safe with him in my house and I did not trust myself with him. All the years of lies and empty promises had me so full of rage. Not anger, but rage.

Three days after that horrific episode I told Mr. LC he had a month to move out. I told him to wait until after the girls were done with school. I think he never thought that I would actually leave him or kick him out for good because we had been there so many times before. He had brought this entire war on himself.

After all he had done, he had the nerve to write me a three-page letter asking me to forgive him and to not give up on our marriage. I was completely convinced he was crazy.

We had set a date to tell the girls about the divorce and the fact that daddy was moving out. I was devastated and confused about how I got to this place. I remember thinking, "*God, am I doing the right thing?*" Dealing with all my trauma and operating in survival mode, it was impossible for me to tell the forest from the trees. Even as a licensed therapist, I did not posses the words to tell my children that their little fairy tale life was over.

You are probably wondering how could I say that after all the drama, especially after everything that had happened the night before my surgery. Well it's because I had spent the last three years damage-controlling their father's bullshit. Their lives didn't change; they still lived in their home, still did their activities — soccer, ballet, Girl Scouts, etc. I sacrificed to ensure they did not go without. They still had American Girl dolls underneath the Christmas tree and extravagant birthday parties. I knew this conversation was going to be difficult. Honestly the only time the girls had ever witnessed us arguing was the night before my surgery.

We all sat down to our family meeting to tell the girls about the divorce. It went something like, "Sometimes big people have big people problems. Daddy is always going to be daddy and mommy is always going to be mommy and we love you and it's not your fault," etc. A very clinical textbook speech was given. All I really remember of that dreadful and sad afternoon is crying with my daughters, especially my oldest. She was a daddy's girl. My little one asked, "So are we still going to Disneyland?" I looked at Mr. LC, and I don't remember who answered, but we said yes. I felt numb inside. From the minute my daughters were born I attempted to create this perfect life for them, a la *The Cosby Show*. When that show was on TV, I thought, *"This show is so fake."* That wasn't my life. I was a black girl born and raised in Newark, New Jersey, to teenage parents. However, as my education level increased and my life experiences grew, I changed my views of the life I could achieve. Thus, my pursuit of a fairy tale life. I strived so hard to be like that perfect family — successful parents, beautiful children, warm home, annual picture perfect Christmas cards, hosting dinner parties. I wondered where did we or I, go wrong?

In June 2009, Mr. LC moved out. There are absolutely no words to describe the relief and joy I felt that day. I felt like a caged animal being set free. In my effort to always put the girls' needs first, I had agreed that I would allow Mr. LC to spend his weekends that he had the girls at the family home in Green Brook. I would just stay with friends or at my mother's house. I had already gotten the girls used to this concept when I introduced them to "daddy-daughter weekend". Remember we had been separated for over a year, but co-habiting. I needed that time to plan, stack my chips, and make sure he didn't completely bail on his responsibility to the girls.

Mr. LC moving out meant I could finally begin to heal myself. It is extremely difficult to begin the healing process when you have to see the person who you perceive is responsible for all your hurt and pain every day. I wanted to pick up of the pieces of my life. I didn't even recognize myself. I had gained so much weight. I felt miserable inside and out. I baked all the time to help deal with my sadness. It was also something I could do with my daughters. Baking was what I did as a child with my paternal grandfather. Mr. LC leaving meant it was my time to be able to talk freely on the phone and have company. Most important, it meant I did not to have to look at his pathetic face.

I was so elated when Mr. LC moved out that I wanted to celebrate. I was turning 33 and decided I would throw myself a "freedom/birthday party." It would be an all-white party. I went all out, especially since Mr. LC did not plan anything for my graduation from graduate school. (Even though two years earlier I had thrown him a huge 40th birthday party at a banquet hall.) I had a DJ, bar, rented patio furniture. I had such a great time. It was a blast. I invited the entire cast of characters in my life. It was a mixture of people from the past and the present. My girl TJ even resurrected Mr. Rico.

Now, you are going to love this one. Mr. LC offered to help me set up for my party and hose down the deck. Against my better judgment, I agreed to let him help me. I later found out he told his family that he came to the party and that we were working things out. I guess he missed the memo that Mr. Rico stayed the night because he was too drunk to drive. I will never understand why he always felt the need to lie about even the smallest things. Further confirmation I was doing the right thing by leaving all the lies behind and moving forward with my life.

Chapter 12

The divorce

Those of us who have lived through a divorce know that it is a daunting, stressful, and emotionally charged process, vacillating between sadness and great anticipation of a better life. Silly me thought my divorce would be relatively smooth. Mr. LC and I had basically agreed that our marriage was not working and we both wanted each other to be happy. We had several conversations about the divorce and wanted to minimize the emotional damage for the girls. Therefore, we both agreed, let's do a "collaborative divorce," move to Los Angeles, and co-parent the girls.

I began the divorce process thinking it should be simple. First I had to find an attorney who had some level of integrity and who would not take me to the cleaners. I did not have $5,000 to spend on legal fees. I always tell people it cost $34 dollars for the marriage license and it costs thousands to get divorced. I went to three free consultations to see what the divorce process would entail. Talk about an invasion of privacy. At each consultation I sat there, and here came 100 questions:

How much do you make?
How much does your husband make?
How much was the house, debt, income, assets?
The list goes on and on…

I didn't feel like any of those lawyers cared about my children or me. More important, I did not want this divorce to drag on for a long period of time. With that said, I decided to go with a family friend. Mainly because I knew she cared that the girls and I were legally protected from fraud with Mr. LC's shady business dealings. I met with her almost a year before I actually filed for divorce.

Ironically, we met at the very same place that I had my engagement party just nine years earlier. We met at Maize, formerly Top Brass, at the Robert Treat Hotel in Newark. If you want to go deeper down the rabbit hole, I used to barmaid there during college. It was a very surreal experience. My heart was heavy. My attorney later told me she questioned whether or not I was really serious about getting divorced. I told her, "Honestly the only thing I ever wanted more than this divorce were my two beautiful daughters." I had finally come to terms with the reality that my marriage was a nightmare that began with lies.

The divorce process began. Of course nothing with Mr. LC was simple. How could it be when he approached every situation with a lie and/or avoidance, as evidenced by him hiding from the legal server not once, but twice? I assumed he thought if he didn't get served it was never going to happen. However, as several divorce lawyers informed me, it takes two people to get married, but only one to get divorced. Thank God for that. My attorney decided she would just go and serve Mr. LC with the divorce papers herself.

I confronted him about this entire situation. He denied all of it. After, he realized he had no choice but to face his reality. I was seriously and actively pursuing a divorce. He finally retained an attorney. My lawyer then forwarded the notice to his attorney. What I thought would be a quick, collaborative divorce turned into a battle. Once he got his attorney, he attempted to prolong the process. My attorney called me one day saying that Mr. LC was contesting the divorce. He wanted equal distributions of the debts and assets. I started crying to my attorney. I said, "What assets? We are behind on both mortgages, our credit card debt is through the roof, and he no longer has the bar." Or so I thought. I later learned that he was still the legal owner of the liquor license. She told me not to worry, we will handle it, but the process will be longer. I hung up the phone and prayed. I needed God to have his hand in the matter.

Everyone told me I needed to fight for half of the bar, the liquor license, and the building. I did not want anything to do with the bar. It was the very thing that destroyed my marriage and family. I repeatedly said to everyone, "God will give me three times more than what I had with Mr. LC." I did not want anything that was associated with him. I waived my right to alimony and his pension. All I wanted was my freedom. No one knew how I had been living in hell with a psychotic liar. People had no idea the pain and emotional abuse I endured from this man. For so many years, he made me think I was crazy. He twisted and manipulated every story, every event and then made me feel crazy when I confronted him with the truth.

For example, while we were going through the divorce I would still speak to his family. We could not believe the lies he told us. One time, he told me he was going to talk to his parents. He came back and said that his mother said it was my fault because I should have never made him buy the house in Green Brook. I found out that same night he never went into their apartment. He just grabbed a plate of food and pulled off. His web of deceit goes on and on. All

I wanted from the divorce was to be legally separated from Mr. LC and gain full custody of my children.

I was told to my face from many friends and family members, "You'll never move to L.A., he won't give you full custody of the girls." I never listened to any of them. I had faith in God. That's all I had was my faith. I had started going to Amanda's church faithfully every Sunday with my daughters. Mr. LC even went with us while we where co-habiting. I would have never made it through the divorce process without God and the power of His word. Religion was no longer a joke for me. I needed the encouragement to believe that I would overcome this nightmare that I created and that life would be better. So while they laughed at me, I continued to plan my move to California. I spoke it into existence in the midst of my trials.

Things were not working with him staying at the house on his weekends with the girls. He was going through my pictures, answering the house phone and going through my belongings. I informed him he could no longer stay at the house. He responded, "It is my house too." I replied, "You lost that privilege when you stopped paying the mortgage, but if you really feel that way I will move out and I want to see you handle the bills and maintenance of this house." He quickly changed his tune. He was in no position to financially afford to live in that house. Mr. LC had finally landed a job. He decided to pursue teaching as career. He taught pre-school, making roughly $18,000 a year. He began taking the girls to his brother's house in Plainfield, New Jersey, when it was his weekend. I needed my space and privacy.

CHAPTER 13

God, please remove this man from my life

I know I said this before, but I wanted Mr. LC out of my life. Even though we were separated and no longer co-habiting, I still saw him every day. Every day when he would pick up and drop off the girls from school, he would find an excuse to come inside the house. I hated his presence. He was always looking around as if someone was going to pop out somewhere. The very fact that he was in my same space annoyed me.

To make matters worse the girls would say, "Daddy are you going to stay for dinner?" He would have a stupid and pathetic look on his face. His response was always, "I don't know, is there enough food for me?" I always replied with the same answer, "Yes I am a Christian, I will feed you dinner." Other times when the girls went upstairs I made comments like, "You didn't come home for dinner when you were fucking your whore." I loved that line; it never got old for me. I used it often. All he ever said in response was, "I'm sorry."

But on a serious note, I knew that my healing, moving on, and letting go of all the painful memories were going to take more than just him not living with me. I needed physical distance and space to heal myself mentally, emotionally, and physically. His daily presence was still taking a toll on my emotional well-being. I was still so angry and full of resentment. I still wasn't sleeping that well and often times crying myself to sleep.

I want to be very clear; I did not want any harm to come to him. I just needed him out of my life for my healing process. On July 27, 2010, the eve of my birthday, I knelt down on my knees and I asked God to remove this man from my life. I was hysterically crying. Even as I was asking God to remove Mr. LC from my life, I thought in my mind, "*Where is he really going to go?*"

Beloved, I'm here to tell you that I serve a powerful and almighty God. The very next day, Mr. LC told me that he "found a job and he was moving far." I said, "Where, Florida?" He replied, "No, Dubai." I said, "Are you serious? That's halfway around the world! What about the girls?" In true Mr. LC fashion he responded with this excuse, "It's a sacrifice to be away from the girls, but it's worth it. I will be able to provide for them in the manner I'm accustomed to doing."

I hung up the phone with Mr. LC. I looked myself in the mirror and realized that when you ask God for something, you do not get the opportunity to say how it's done or when it happens. As so many times before, I was ambivalent. I knew I wanted him away from me, but I knew the girls were going to struggle with not seeing their father and him being so far away. More important, I knew from that moment on I was going to be a single parent. I found myself in my mother's shoes, some twenty years later — a mother struggling to raise her two children by herself.

I had to trust God. I knew that it was all part of His plan for me. In his typical selfish manner, Mr. LC told me he was scheduled to leave within the next three weeks — just another example of him dropping a bombshell on me. Once again, we would sit the girls down to talk about his departure to Dubai. I do not recall any of the words he said to Sarah and Victoria. I told him prior to our conversation with the girls, "This is your choice, your decision, you tell the girls. As always I will pick up the pieces of their little broken hearts." Of course the girls sobbed hysterically. They could not understand why their father was moving halfway around the world. I cried with them because I felt their pain. As their mother I wanted to shield my children from all of life's pain. I had damaged-controlled so much of Mr. LC's bullshit. This was out of my control. Also, truthfully, what I had asked God for.

He had told me that he was going to learn Spanish and finish his master's program while in Dubai. (Please remember this detail for later). He said these things would make him more marketable in the workforce once he returned to the states. So on August 18, 2010, the girls and I drove Mr. LC to JFK airport. I remember crying on the drive back from the airport. My thoughts were, "*Can I do this alone? Can I raise these girls alone?*"

So many times during our marriage, Mr. LC showed me that he was a coward. He was leaving now under the guise of "a sacrifice." The reality was he was running away because he was embarrassed by the loss of his family, his business, his beloved Yukon Denali, his wife, and two homes.

With all this going on, I had gotten laid off from the public school system. In addition to having my two daughters to take care of physically and emotionally, I had the daunting task of trying to find a job. I applied to everything and anything. I remember telling my mother that I never have to look hard for a job. I didn't get one call, one interview — nothing. I thought, "*How can this be? I have a master's degree!*"

On a positive note, I was able to be there for the girls. Being home allowed me to do the school drop off and pick up for the entire month of September. I was grateful for Amanda. She was there helping me with the girls and provided emotional support for me. Amanda kept saying, "Don't worry, God is going to work this out for you." It was difficult to have that faith when the reality of my bills and life were overwhelming.

However, Mr. LC leaving eventually gave me the biggest sense of relief. I needed this to heal and move on. I was grateful to have a sense of peace for the first time in so many years. Now my focus was helping the girls adjust to life without their father. I informed their teachers of the situation regarding Mr. LC being in Dubai. In nice suburban Green Brook, I heard over and over, *"Oh, you poor thing, let me know what I can do for you or the girls."* Why do people say things they do not mean?

Truly, my life is a testimony of God's grace. I received a call from the school district. They offered me two positions to choose from. Later that same day I got a call from an agency for a per diem in-home counseling job. In October of 2010, I was back to work. My faith taught me God knows everything. He knew my girls needed me home that first month of school. They needed my physical presence to reassure them that I was there. God's grace even had my position be from 10 a.m. to 5 p.m., so I was able to take the girls to school and then go to work. It was a perfect fit.

Although I finally had physical space from Mr. LC, I was still legally married. I wanted this ordeal to be over. My attorney confirmed that he did not need to be present for the final court date. On October 18, 2010, I went to court alone. I was dressed in one of my best suits and planned on going to work after court. Due to a situation beyond her control, my attorney was running late. It was a surreal experience to sit in the courtroom listening to the dissolution of other people's marriages. There was absolutely no privacy. Funny how when you are getting married everyone refers to it as a holy and sacred union. Well, that all changes by the time you are in divorce court. It basically turns into a public display of failure for everyone sitting in the courts.

As I sat there, I almost couldn't believe it was finally happening. I had filed for divorce over a year prior. All I wanted was my freedom from Mr. LC, the man who had caused me so much hurt and pain. I knew that if I didn't get divorced then, I would have died in that marriage at an early age. As the judge called my case I felt a knot in my stomach, and I was nauseous. Within moments of the judge reviewing my divorce decree, and a simple, "Yes your honor, no your honor," I was divorced. My fairy tale was over. I left the courthouse, turned to my attorney and said, 'It's over, I'm free." She said, "Yes you are; go enjoy life."

Enjoying my life meant one thing to me: moving to California. Remember, prior to Mr. LC leaving for Dubai, we had agreed to move to L.A. and co-parent the girls. People always ask, "Why California?" I had wanted to go to college in California. My mother told me if I stayed in New Jersey she would buy me a car. So of course I stayed, but never got the car. It was my dream to live in L.A. I was doing this for me, Grace. I had sacrificed so much being in that marriage. I had given up my 20s and early 30s to be a wife and a mother. This was the one thing I could do for myself. It was a chance to restart my life.

All the haters repeatedly said, "You're not moving to L.A.," primarily because of the custody issue with my children. But God worked that out for me and without a fight. When Mr. LC decided to leave the country I was awarded sole custody of my daughters. Therefore I was free to move anywhere I wanted. Secondly, I assume the haters thought that I wasn't strong enough to leave the comfort of everything I've ever known; my house, job, friends, social life, etc.

There was no incentive to stay in New Jersey. I had no help from my family. I'm not referring to money. I'm talking about emotional support. I had people who promised to take the girls one weekend a month, which never happened one time. I had a father who used my house as a hotel. When he could not afford the gas in his BMW X5 to get back and forth to his house in Pennsylvania, he would stay at my house. This went on for a couple of months. He would stay two to three times a week. He never once helped me rake a leaf, shovel after one snowstorm, or any other normal things a father does for his daughter. Once he got a new car, he stopped coming over. He had always disappointed my brother and me our entire lives. I asked my father not to let the girls down by just stopping to come over. But he did not care. I figured if I'm going to be a single mother I'd rather be in beautiful southern California. Also, in my heart I felt I could provide a better life for my girls.

The only person who helped me was my best friend, Lydia. She and I went through our divorces at the same time. We had become each other's rock. We would take turns hosting each other's kids, five in total, just to give each other a break from motherhood. At different points during our divorces, we offered each other the opportunity to live together. I offered when Lydia was selling her marital home and looking for a new home. Lydia offered when the financial overhead of my house was like a rope around my neck. In the end, it worked out for the both of us. I know that no matter where we live, we will be BFFs and as Lydia calls us "sistahs from different mothers."

I also had the gift of Amanda's friendship. I became even more overwhelmed with my reality of money issues, single parenthood — not to mention our age difference. Amanda and I were over as lovers. We remained really good friends. I believe that people come into your life for a reason and a season. She was instrumental in helping me grow deeper with God.

I relied on her for her spiritual words of encouragement and her constant support of my dreams. She was a blessing to my daughters. Her love for them was unconditional. I will forever have a special place in my heart for her. I tell everyone, Amanda was there for me during my divorce, when "friends" I had know for over fifteen years turned their backs on my children and me.

Moreover there was no more time for distractions. I needed to focus my attention, time, and energy with planning my move to California. I had the task of moving across the country with two young children. This was going to be a major life change for all of us. The goal was to provide the easiest transition for my daughters, never losing sight of wanting the very best for them and their future. I researched school districts, diverse neighborhoods, and where to set up my private practice. More important than my own research, I prayed and inquired of the Lord. I asked God to guide my footsteps with my plan to move to Los Angeles.

CHAPTER 14

Time, turn, and tenacity

Now, it's 2011 and I am still executing my plan to move to L.A. I stayed in constant prayer, asking God to give me the wisdom to make the best decisions for my family. Even with help from Lydia and Amanda, I was worn out from being a single mom. I was becoming concerned with how was I going to be able to find a job and take care of the girls in California with no support system. I began to have self-doubt. I needed a backup plan. I thought a possible option would be to send the girls to Dubai with their father for a school year. That would enable me to get things settled in L.A. faster.

After wanting nothing more than getting away from that habitual liar, I actually entertained the thought of going to Dubai. The plan would be for me live with Mr. LC for three to four months and get the girls settled. Then I would head to L.A. Sounds like a good plan, right? My daughters would have an international experience and live with their father again. I would be able to get settled in and prepare a home for them in Los Angeles.

So, with reservation, I went to Dubai in June of 2011 to see if I could see the girls living there in my absence. Dubai was exotic and absolutely amazing. Mr. LC was the same. While I was there he took me to a comedy show. I thought "*I can't go back to living with him.*" With all his free time he had joined a comedy group. He hadn't changed one bit. Mr. LC left stating he was going to rebuild himself, grow deeper with God, focus on his career, learn Spanish, and complete an online graduate degree. I wasn't there more than three days before I realized, "I can't go back!"

That plan was short-lived. I jumped on a plane back to New Jersey. It was absolutely insane to have I thought I could co-habit with that man again. I truly must have lost my mind with the stress of working two jobs, taking care of the girls, and maintaining the house. God, delivered not once but *twice* from the enemy! Although I had already decided Dubai was not an option for my daughters or me, Mr. LC ended up writing me a letter stating he couldn't have me come live with him if we were not getting back together. I thought to myself, "*You must be crazy if you think I would get back with you after I found extra small tighty-whities in your nightstand.*"

Not to mention, he always wore boxers. (Read in between the lines.) When I confronted him, he had the same lying expression I had seen in the previous ten years. Mr. LC said, "I bought the wrong size." That was my sign to exit stage left immediately! Or should I say exit Dubai.

Now back to reality. I had visited L.A. several times with Mr. LC while we were married. I had also gone solo to look at schools, as well as vacationed with Amanda. I had consulted my uncle for many aspects concerning the move, given he had moved with his wife to California for her job some seven years earlier. The plan was to live with my uncle, his wife, and their son while I got on my feet. I needed to determine where exactly I wanted to re-establish myself in L.A.

My uncle had a history of renting rooms out of his home. We agreed in the beginning of the conversations regarding the move that I would have two bedrooms; one for me and one for the girls to share. I knew he was going to charge me rent; I never expected to live there rent-free. I told him that while I could not afford to pay $800 a month (his standard rental fee) I could afford $500, plus buy my own food. I thought that was more than fair considering I was moving with no job. He told me not to worry, "We will make it work."

Less than two weeks before I was scheduled to get on a plane with my two children he sent me an email. The email basically stated, if I could not or was not willing to pay him the $800 a month, then my children and I could not move into his home. Additionally, he proceeded to list my options, one of which included staying in New Jersey.

I was shocked by his cavalier behavior. At this point, my back was against the wall. I had gotten laid off again from the school district due to budget cuts, my house was packed up, and I had moved everything into storage. Flights were already purchased. All I could do was drop to my knees and pray to God. I opened my Bible and read Psalm 37. I started crying and said, "God, I will only go if you give me three signs by tomorrow." God gave me my three signs. I went on faith, trusting only in His word and grace.

I let Amanda and Lydia read the email. They were both disgusted that a family member could write such a callous email. Each of them, having faith in me, said, "Go, you will make it." My uncle had already prepped my mother, and she said I should go as well.

It's one thing when people in the world screw you over, but it's completely heartbreaking when your own family screws you over. My uncle wasn't the first and won't be the last. I believe God allowed that to happen so his real personality could be revealed to me.

I am going to be the bigger person and not elaborate on the entire experience of living in that house. However, I will repeat what my oldest daughter always says, "They were not nice to us." My darling, that is putting it mildly. We endured them eating our food and not replacing it. Their son, Jalin, throwing Victoria's books out. Jalin telling the girls, "This is my house," and so many other un-Christian acts. Through that very painful but powerful lesson, I became stronger and my children learned to be resilient.

Despite that uninviting welcome, being in California was a dream come true. It wasn't exactly what I expected at first. I was not living in Los Angeles County. My uncle lived all the way in Ventura County. We were at least a solid hour away from Studio City, Beverly Hills, West Hollywood, or any other area closer to L.A. It was an adjustment coming from living in my huge house to literally being cramped into one bedroom. I knew that I wasn't going to stay there long. I had traded Green Brook, New Jersey for Simi Valley, California. I wanted diversity and a hipster L.A. vibe. I wanted to see the sights. Instead, I got boring small town.

Luckily, I had a friend, Kathy, who lived in L.A. She was gracious enough to give me keys to her apartment. Kathy had lived with my uncle on two separate occasions when she was relocating from New Jersey. She understood firsthand the bullshit that a person had to deal with living with my uncle, so every weekend I packed the girls up and we headed into Los Angeles. We crashed at her place. I slept on the couch and the girls on the air mattress. We didn't care; we were comfortable at Kathy's. Every weekend was like a little adventure. We went to The Grove, LACMA, Paradise Cove, and so many other cool spots. I was so grateful and appreciative for Kathy. She was the peace in the midst of my storm.

Due to the distance and logistics I didn't even bother to look for work. There was no way to work and be able to pick up and drop off the girls every day. I had no help from my uncle. Bertha, his wife, was no mother to her own son. So I sure as hell wasn't counting on her. This is the same woman who threw her son's artwork in the trash right in front of him. Most parents usually put that stuff on the fridge. Well, to each its own. The girls were blessed with amazing teachers and friends while we lived in Simi Valley. Kathy kept saying, "This is only temporary."

I used my time there to establish my business in California. I located my first office space, created my website, had business cards made. I was preparing myself for success. I used any opportunity to network and meet people. I joined social work organizations and found a volunteer organization to give of my talents. My main focus was on taking care of the girls. I knew that it was an adjustment for me, so I could only imagine what they were feeling. We continued their activities, and added new ones. They were doing OK, but I knew they missed New Jersey and their family. They were my motivation for everything.

My tenacity and vision for success paid off. Eight months after I landed in Los Angeles, I had moved into a condo with Kathy and the girls, had my office on the west side, and started seeing clients. I had even landed a job providing therapy in a youth homeless shelter. I stayed faithful to God's promise for my life in California. Despite the painful transition of moving across the country, missing my friends and the comforts of my home, I saw the bigger picture. I listened to the voice of God when he said, "For I know the plans I have for you … plans to give you hope and a future." (Jeremiah 29:11 NIV)

CHAPTER 15

Comedy and closure

In the summer of 2012, Mr. LC moved to California. When Mr. LC moved to L.A., people thought it was to be closer to his daughters. I knew before he landed at LAX. He wasn't moving to be closer for the girls. If that were the case he would have never left them. The truth is he moved to L.A. to pursue comedy and acting. His Twitter account states he also does voice-over. Yes, comedy is meant to be funny. It's actually not funny when you haven't been in the same country as your daughters for two years and you put going on auditions over spending time with them. There were so many days that I asked him, "Can you pick up the girls from school or watch them while I see clients?" He would always answer that he was working his security job. Days later I'd see pictures of him on his Facebook in a Superman costume. (No, we are not Facebook friends; Kathy would show me) Another time, it was his weekend to spend time with the girls. He called and asked if I could watch them because he had an audition for a sneaker commercial. I replied via text, "You can pursue your bullshit on your own time." He response was, "A national sneaker commercial is not bullshit." Needless to say he didn't get that gig.

I saw two tapes of his comedy act when I was in Dubai. Let's just say he's no Kevin Hart. I could not believe he actually had the nerve to get on stage. However, I want to be clear about Mr. LC. This was not his first unrealistic endeavor in the entertainment industry. When we first met, he was managing his brother's rap group. Then he was trying to work with another artist who had a rock band. And right as his portion of the bar was falling apart, he decided to start managing a boxer. He made countless trips to L.A. to attend the boxer's fights. So, you see Mr. LC had a long history of chasing the Hollywood dream, none of which had ever proven to be successful.

I found nothing funny or comical when he stopped paying child support. Nor when he moved in with my uncle and paid him $800 a month for a room. Nothing was funny about him not working a regular job to support his daughters. I emailed Mr. LC several times that his daughters were crying and missing him. It was easier for my daughters to understand when Daddy was in Dubai why they didn't see him. But now Daddy was in California, not more than 25 miles away. When I informed him that the girls where crying for him, he said, "Have them call me." I responded, "They do; you don't answer your phone." So by his actions, he proved he didn't move to California for his daughters. If he did they would have never felt a void of his presence in their lives while he resided in the same state.

However, I do know what is funny. That would be social media. He would plaster his page with pictures of their soccer games and school awards. He would take pictures that depicted him being a "good father." In reality the minute the photo opportunity was over, I got a text saying, "What time will you be home so I can drop off the girls?" If I had a quarter for every time he asked me that, I'd be rich. One day I actually timed him; he had the girls for less than three hours. His Facebook page read the same day, "Nothing better than spending the day with my girls." Actually, I take that back, it's not funny — it's pathetic. Pathetic that people use these tools to promote or brag about their fake lives knowing it's all a lie.

Perhaps Mr. LC wanted to use comedy to escape his reality. I know that feeling; I had been there myself. Life taught me if you do not deal with your current situation you can't heal or move on. If you continue to do the same dysfunctional things — lie, steal, cheat, or pretend shit is not real — there is no peace. The Bible says, "A double minded man is unstable in all his ways." (James 1:8 KJV). A friend once asked me, "Why do you keep having hope that he (Mr. LC) will change?"

I responded simply, "Because my children deserve better." Honestly, Mr. LC deserves a better life. Unfortunately, as his grandmother taught me, "You can't want for people what they don't want for themselves."

Closure means that you have processed the event and learned the lessons and seek to move on with life. There are days when I believe that my closure was the divorce, or that fact that I am living in California. The reality is that chapter of my life is over. Having told my story brings me closure. Truly, it's extremely difficult or perhaps impossible to bring full closure when you have two children with that person. Those children who need that very part of your life that you otherwise would have nothing to do with. Mr. LC is and will always be their father. I feel compelled to say that this book is not about him, his actions, or lack thereof.

You see, Mr. LC and I lost the same things. We lost homes, cars, the business, money, exotic vacations, and all the other things I lamented when they were gone.

Sadly, he lost something he can never get back: his family. That's not my story. I lost "stuff" but gained freedom, peace, and happiness. I have the kisses before bedtime, the girls' artwork all over the house. I get to see my ballerina twirl around because she doesn't have a care in the world. I get to experience my little engineer growing smarter than me by the day. This is my reality and it is priceless.

CHAPTER 16

Reconstructive Realness

We live in a world where everyone wants the quick fix. I spent years cultivating my fairy tale life. When the fairy tale was over I had to recreate my life, myself and redefine who I truly was, or should I say the person I wanted to become. So many people ask, "How did you rebuild yourself?" I wish I could say I went to some exotic island, became a vegan, and did yoga three times a day. But that's only in the movies. I literally had to pick up the pieces of my life. It was a painful and sobering experience. If I truly wanted to be happy and rebuild my life, it meant I had to rid myself of all the shame, guilt, and anger.

My journey to peace meant I had to be honest with myself. I had to really take a long hard look in the mirror. "*Who was this woman? How did I go from being a fiercely independent woman to this pathetic shell of myself?*" I spent my entire life being a people pleaser. Wanting desperately the approval of my mother and others. I did this to a fault. I prided myself on being the "bigger person" and "doing the right thing," even if that meant I had to sacrifice who I was or want I wanted.

I felt I had no right to complain about my dysfunctional childhood and the abuse I suffered because I had become successful. I didn't want anyone to know my truth — my crazy, my insecurities, my struggles. I didn't want people to think less of my abilities or me. I lived my life even from childhood with a smile on my face, despite whatever was going on with me or at home. I later learned in therapy that suppressing my feelings was wrong and it did more damage than good.

How was I expected to go ten years without any contact from my father and pretend that I was "fine"? I learned to create a fairy tale life from my family.

It didn't matter what was going on inside, as long as I/ we looked good from the outside. My paternal grandfather would say over and over again "loose lips sink ships." As a child that meant one thing: "Keep your mouth shut." So the violence, the drugs, the yelling, and screaming are all OK as long as no one knows. And when morning comes, we won't speak on it because it never happened.

For years this was the cycle; chaotic and violent nights followed by quiet and sober mornings. I would wake up, put my smile on my face, and then go to school. At school I was the honor student, the good girl. I excelled — it was my escape. As I got older, I knew that if I could just get to college I could leave all the madness behind me. I could live my life on my terms.

In addition to pretending that life was great all the time, I modeled all the toxic relationships that played out in front of me. My abandonment issues created unhealthy relationships with older men. Whenever I felt like they were leaving, I left them first. Then it was on to the next one.

Back then I never even knew what I was looking for in a man or a relationship. What mattered was that they could take care of me. And with every gift and expensive dinner, it proved just how much they loved and wanted me. Now looking back, I wanted someone to love me for "who I was." Not just love my face, my body, or how they would look with me on their arm. I wanted to feel special and different. When Mr. LC came along, I thought I had found that person.

I learned that when I decided to create my fairy tale life with Mr. LC I really just traded my dysfunctional childhood storyline for the adult version. I have said it before: I knew I should not have married him. I felt the need to save face and "do the right thing."

In my journey to rebuilding myself, I found an amazing therapist who helped me see all the dysfunctional patterns in my life. I was able to recognize I was playing out the adult version of my childhood. It was now me who was yelling and screaming at night, then waking up and pretending it never happened. I was in a chaotic, toxic marriage, and I was hurting. I couldn't tell anyone because from the outside we were a beautiful family and had a good life. So I smiled and made it look fabulous with the trips, dinner parties, and lavish gifts. I distracted myself with an affair, because the pain of my husband's cheating and my failing marriage was too much for me to bear.

I was hurt, ashamed, and embarrassed that it was I who created this life. I was angry with myself for doing this to my daughters and me. I was angry that my parents were not there for me when I was a child and still now even as an adult. In therapy I learned to forgive and love myself. I learned that when you love yourself, you do not allow people to use, abuse, or disrespect you. I learned that I was deserving of true love that wasn't tainted with lies.

I found comfort in knowing that I wasn't all to blame for this mess I created. Nor do I seek to blame anyone else. The reality is we are the sum total of our life experiences. My experiences in my childhood allowed me to view the decisions I made as "normal." However, the growth and the rebuilding come into play when we as adults come to that fork in the road: We can either play victim to our past and faults and stay in pity mode or we can learn the lessons and rise above the obstacles.

My choice to leave my marriage was a defining moment in my life. At one point I told my therapist, "Maybe I can stay there until Sarah goes to college?" She looked at me and said, "At what cost?" I answered, "It doesn't matter, I have lost everything." It wasn't that I still valued the illusion of my fairy tale. But rather, I was afraid. I spent my life being afraid of the unknown, afraid of being alone, afraid of failure.

I learned to break away from living in fear. I learned that when you operate from a place of fear it robs you and your family of living an authentic life. Fear kills dreams, destroys relationships, and stunts your growth. I rebuilt my life by learning to walk in faith. When I let go of being anxious, I learned how strong I was. It meant learning to truly pray and trust God. By focusing on God and through His power, I was able to be restored. I had to do my part; whether that was raking leaves, shoveling snow, and/or raising my girls alone. I knew that it would be through Christ who strengthens me that I could do whatever I needed to do in life. Not only would I overcome; I would be better than I ever was before. I knew that God loved me. (And for the first time I loved myself.)

Reconstructing my life meant that I had to protect my heart, value the person I truly was, and be proud of the person I had become as a result of this experience. I had become a strong, emotionally mature, complex but well—grounded woman.

I eliminated people in my life who were negative and filled my head with doubt or confusion. By cutting certain friends and family members out of my life I was able to stay positive and focus on my dreams. Choosing to only associate and share my feelings with my true friends allowed me to cultivate a circle of love for my daughters and myself. I learned through that fairy tale marriage that I would not allow people to hurt me and then keep them around, even if they were related to me. As they say, "Misery loves company."

I am constantly changing and growing. I found that I had to surround myself with other positive and progressive people. People who could share my vision of a brighter future and success.

I tell my story to motivate, encourage, and give hope to people. Life is going to knock you down, and perhaps strip you down to nothing. And it's gonna hurt like hell. You are going to lose friends, family members, material things, status, jobs, money — and the list goes on. But do not give up! There is a lesson in every trial, disappointment, and tribulation.

Today, I am truly happy and secure in who I am. My clients always ask, "If you could do it all over again knowing what you know now, would you?" My answer, without hesitation is, "Yup, in a New York minute. It was all part of the process to get me to this moment in life."

With that said I leave you with my personal mantra for life and what I tell my clients: "*Life is a collection of experiences; learn and grow. Be stronger and wiser.*"

The End

About the Author

Grace Carrington is a Life Coach specializing in individual, adolescent and couples counseling, and maintains a private practice in Southern California. Ms. Carrington holds a Master's degree in Clinical Social Work. Among her areas of expertise are relationship issues, parent coaching, divorce recovery, woman's issues, and LBGTQ community issues.

Grace is an interactive and solution-focused coach. Her role is to provide support and practical feedback to help clients effectively address personal life challenges. Ms. Carrington integrates compassion, cultural sensitivity and humor as she works with each client to empower themselves to make healthy life choices for an abundant and authentic life. To contact Ms. Carrington, please visit her website www.chatlifecoaching.com.

Made in the USA
Las Vegas, NV
07 February 2022

43339968R00052